To:

From:

fatherhood
is not for sissies

COMPILED BY

Evelyn Beilenson

 PETER PAUPER PRESS, INC.
White Plains, New York

For my father, who was always there for me

Designed by Heather Zschock

Photo Credits appear on page 72.

Copyright © 2007
Peter Pauper Press, Inc.
202 Mamaroneck Avenue
White Plains, NY 10601
All rights reserved
ISBN 978-1-59359-855-6
6 5 4 3 2 1
Printed in China

Visit us at www.peterpauper.com

fatherhood

is not for sissies

introduction

Fatherhood is not for sissies. What other job description requires a 24/7 commitment the likes of which only a parent can imagine? Take any other job. Then supersize it. And supersize it again. OK, you get the picture. This new little bundle of joy needs to be fed, burped, diapered, clothed, played with, taught

the meaning of right and wrong . . . and most of all, loved and hugged, spit-up and all. And no one can do that like Dad can.

Fathers are the gentle giants who offer protection and patience. As has been said, *Every cub is the king of the jungle in his father's eyes.*

Dads are there for comfort when things go bump in the night; for fun when things go *vroom* in the driveway; and later for support and counsel when the going gets tough. At the end of the day, there's no other job quite as important or satisfying.

This book's for you, Dad. We hope you'll enjoy knowing that you're not alone as you face the trials of fatherhood, and reflecting on all the funny moments involved in raising kids. And, most of all, we hope you'll know just how loved and appreciated you are.

Here's to you, Dad.
You're the Man!

I had heard all those things
about fatherhood, how
great it is. But it's greater
than I'd ever expected—
I had no idea Quinton
would steal my heart the
way he has. From the
minute I laid eyes on him,
I knew nobody could ever
wrestle him away from me.

BURT REYNOLDS

I felt something impossible
for me to explain in words. Then
when they took her away, it hit me.
I got scared all over again and
began to feel giddy. Then it came
to me—I was a father.

NAT KING COLE

A father today has disposable diapers and plastic bottles. The only thing left to invent is a plastic toy that will hit the floor and then bounce back into the crib.

BILL COSBY

*A father finds out what is meant by
"a spitting image" when he tries
to feed cereal to an infant.*

IMOGENE FEY

When Dad can't get the diaper on straight, we laugh at him as though he were trying to walk around in high-heel shoes. Do we ever assist him by pointing out that all you have to do is lay out the diaper like a baseball diamond, put the kid's butt on the pitcher's mound, bring home plate up, then fasten the tapes at first and third base?

MICHAEL K. MEYERHOFF

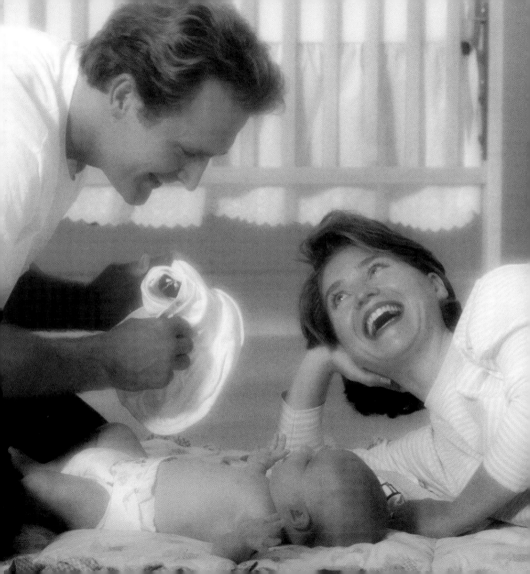

When Charles first saw our child Mary,
he said all the proper things
for a new father. He looked upon
the poor little red thing and blurted,
"She's more beautiful
than the Brooklyn Bridge."

HELEN HAYES

It's a glorious day when a father is born.

BARBARA PAULDING

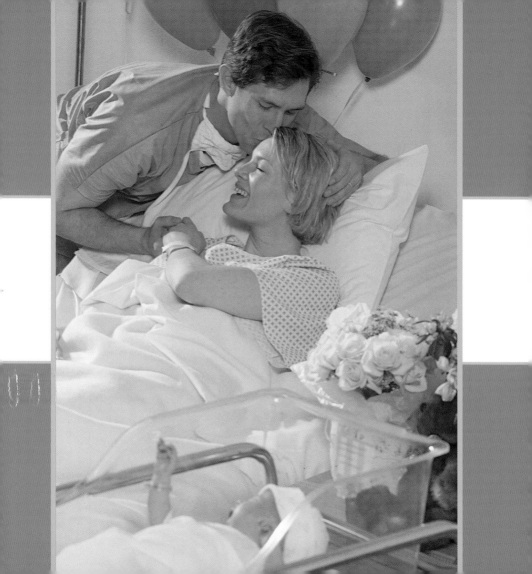

Raising kids is part joy and part guerrilla warfare.

ED ASNER

To become a father
is not hard;
to be a father is,
however.

WILHELM BUSCH

A baby has a way
of making a man out of
his father and a boy out
of his grandfather.

ANGIE PAPADAKIS

There are times when parenthood seems nothing but feeding the mouth that bites you.

PETER DE VRIES

Children are natural
mimics—they
act like their fathers
or mothers in spite of
every attempt to teach
them good manners.

AUTHOR UNKNOWN

*There are only two lasting bequests
we can hope to give our children.
One of these is roots; the other, wings.*

HODDING CARTER

The million-dollar smile
doesn't come cheap.

The child had
every toy his
father wanted.

ROBERT C. WHITTEN

One father is
more than a hundred
schoolmasters.

ENGLISH PROVERB

Dad—ask him when Mom says no.

AUTHOR UNKNOWN

The real menace in dealing with a five-year-old is that in no time at all you begin to sound like a five-year-old.

JEAN KERR

I have found the best way to give advice to your children is to find out what they want and then advise them to do it.

Children are supposed to
help hold a marriage
together. They do
this in a number of ways.
For instance, they demand
so much attention that
a husband and wife,
concentrating on their
children, fail to notice
each other's faults.

RICHARD ARMOUR

Before I got married, I had six theories about bringing up children. Now I have six children and no theories.

JOHN WILMOT

Children need love, especially when they do not deserve it.

HAROLD HULBERT

Steve was terrible in chemistry and I'd try helping him with his homework. Once, when he got a D in the subject, he came home and said, "Dad, you flunked."

ARNOLD SPIELBERG

My father used to play with
my brother and me in the yard.
Mother would come out and say,
"You're tearing up the grass."
"We're not raising grass,"
Dad would reply.
"We're raising boys."

HARMON KILLEBREW

People who say
they sleep like
babies usually
don't have them.

LEO J. BURKE

I cannot think of any
need in childhood
as strong as the need for
a father's protection.

SIGMUND FREUD

A father is always making his baby into a little woman. And when she is a woman he turns her back again.

ENID BAGNOLD

One night a father
overheard his son pray,
"Dear God,
Make me the kind of
man my Daddy is."
Later that night,
a father prayed,
"Dear God,
Make me the kind of
man my son wants
me to be."

AUTHOR UNKNOWN

Every cub is the
king of the jungle
in his father's eyes.

Who said tackling
fatherhood would
be glamorous?

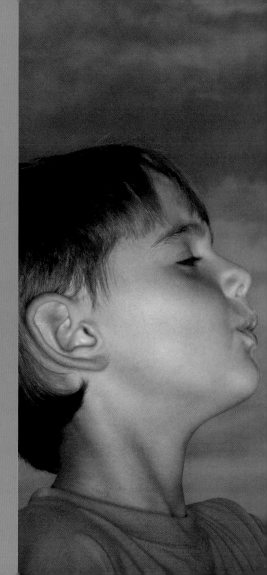

You can learn
many things from
children. How
much patience you
have, for instance.

FRANKLIN P. JONES

You know your
children are growing
up when they stop
asking you where
they came from and
refuse to tell you
where they're going.

P. J. O'ROURKE

If you can give
your son or
daughter only
one gift, let it
be enthusiasm.

BRUCE BARTON

photo credits